The Man-Eating Tigers of Sundarbans

The Man-Eating Tigers of Sundarbans

Sy Montgomery

with photographs by Eleanor Briggs

Houghton Mifflin Company   Boston

For Girindra,

amar boro bhai,

and his family

Text copyright © 2001 by Sy Montgomery
Photographs copyright © 2001 by Eleanor Briggs

www.houghtonmifflinbooks.com

Book design by Lisa Diercks
The text of this book is set in Columbus and Humana Script.

Library of Congress Cataloging-in-Publication Data

Montgomery, Sy.
The man-eating tigers of Sundarbans / Sy Montgomery ; photographs by Eleanor Briggs.
p.   cm.
Includes bibliographical references (p.).
RNF ISBN 0-618-07704-9   PAP ISBN 0-618-49490-1
1. Tigers — Sundarbans (Bangladesh and India) — Juvenile literature. 2. Dangerous animals —
Sundarbans (Bangladesh and India) — Juvenile literature. [1. Tigers. 2. Sundarbans (Bangladesh and India)]
I. Briggs, Eleanor, ill. II. Title.
QL737.C23 M66   2001
599.756'0954'14 — dc21
00-32031

Printed in Singapore
TWP 10 9 8 7 6 5 4 3 2

the Tiger Is Watching

A warm May night in eastern India is a peaceful time in the mud-and-thatch villages that ring the forest at the edge of the sea. The farmers have returned from working in their gardens and rice fields. The children are back from school and now recite their evening lessons or chant prayers. The air carries the cozy scent of wood smoke, baking bread, and spicy stews bubbling over clay hearths. It is a good time to be home.

But it is not a good time to be out in a boat on the rivers and channels that thread through the forest. Young Golam was nervous.

Golam and his four friends were far from their village. They were deep inside the tiger reserve. They weren't supposed to be there. The five young men were breaking the law. But they had come anyway, in search of beehives full of sweet, spicy honey, which they planned to collect and sell at the markets.

They anchored their little wooden boat in the river. They would sleep on the boat,

surrounded by the river, the forest, and the night sky. They knew this was dangerous as well as illegal. To calm themselves, the five chatted on the deck while the last light faded.

"If we find some honey, what price do you think we will get for it at the market?" Golam said to his friend Deben, who was sitting next to him in the dark.

There was no answer.

"Deben?"

Then everyone heard a splash.

The men shouted and scrambled onto the deck of the small boat. They grabbed for the flashlight. Finally, someone shined the light on the muddy bank of the river. There, caught in its beam, was a huge, wet tiger — carrying Deben's body by the back of the neck, the way a cat carries a mouse!

How had it happened?

It seemed impossible. Silently, the tiger had swum up to the boat. Without making a sound, without rocking the boat, the giant cat had leapt from the water onto the little wooden craft. No one had felt the tiger's presence as it walked, inches from the other men, to grab Deben by the back of the neck. No one had felt the boat dip when the tiger leapt off the boat with the body of their companion and slipped back into the water.

Elsewhere in the world, tigers almost never attack people—much less kill and eat them. And yet this is what the four men left on the boat knew had happened. They had heard stories about tiger attacks many times before.

By the light of the flashlight, Golam and his friends saw the tiger melt into the forest with their friend in its mouth. Deben was never seen again.

Is this what *really* happened?

Are the tigers who live in this forest different from other tigers? Why do they hunt people? Do these tigers really have powers other tigers don't? And what about the stories people tell—are they true? If the tigers are so dangerous, why don't the people just kill them all or move away?

A few scientists and wildlife managers have long pondered questions about the tigers who live in this giant forest by the sea. So much about this unusual forest and its fierce tigers remains mysterious.

If you like mysteries, maybe these are some you'd like to solve.

Perhaps you could find some clues from learning about the forest in which these strange tigers live. Is there something about this place that might cause the tigers to behave so strangely?

Perhaps you might also try to track the tigers. You could follow their footprints to find out where they go and what they do and compare your answers with the ways tigers live in other places. Do they differ from other tigers in their habits as well as their unusual appetites?

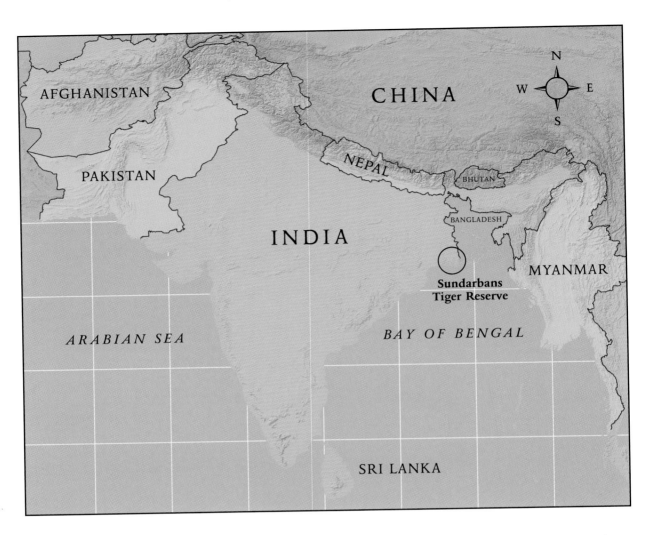

Surely you would want to talk to the people who live in this forest. You could ask them questions and write down their stories. Why do they choose to live in a place full of man-eating tigers?

Maybe you would want to do all of these things. And maybe some of the answers would lead to even *more* mysteries.

Where to begin? First, you would have to fly halfway around the world. To get ready, you would need shots against tropical diseases such as yellow fever, encephalitis, hepatitis, and cholera. Where you're going there are no hospitals, and though the shots are no fun, they'll help protect you from getting sick.

Your plane might land in Dacca, the capital of the country of Bangladesh, or you might fly into Calcutta, the capital of the state of West Bengal in eastern India. From there you

The port city of Canning.

would take a bus or a train or a car to one of the ports on the Bay of Bengal. In India, that might be a city called Canning; in Bangladesh, it might be the town of Bagherhat, which means "tiger market" in Bengali, the language spoken there. (It would be a good idea to learn some Bengali before you left, because outside the big cities, almost nobody speaks English.)

And here you would leave cars behind. You can get to the tigers' forest only by boat. There are no roads, only waterways—and both the land and the waters can be extremely dangerous.

Your travels won't always be easy or comfortable. Be sure to bring water. You can't drink the river water; it's full of mud and salt. Take a flashlight: there is no electricity,

except for the occasional village generator. If you want to communicate with people at home, bring paper and envelopes, because there are no telephones. Even the mail sometimes takes a month to be delivered.

Be ready for changes in weather. From late March to late May, there are sudden rainstorms and sometimes hail. Then there are three months of almost constant rain. So pack a raincoat. The dry season—late September to March—is hot during the day, with sweater-cool nights. The glare on the water can hurt your eyes, so bring sunglasses and a hat with a wide brim, as well as long-sleeved shirts and long pants so you won't get sunburned. But don't come in October—that's when there might be terrible winds called cyclones. Small animals can be blown for miles, and whole houses break apart!

There's another problem, too:

Your study subject might be trying to eat you!

A Visit to Sundarbans

Along the Bay of Bengal, between the countries of India and Bangladesh, stretches this strange and beautiful flooded forest, part ocean, part river, part trees.

In the rivers live pink dolphins. On the beaches, giant turtles dig nests in which to lay their eggs. In the forests live delicate spotted deer called chital, big hairy hogs called wild boar—and more tigers than anywhere else on earth. There are said to be some five hundred tigers here.

As you travel the waterways in your boat, you will find their footprints everywhere. There, in the wet mud of the riverbank, you can see where a huge tiger hauled itself out of the water! You can even see where the tiger extended its great claws to keep from slipping in the mud. The sandy beaches are criss-crossed with the footprints of tigers, too. Sometimes you will find the footprints of a big tiger with those of two little ones: a mother and her cubs.

Sometimes you can find tiger footprints on ground where there were none only five minutes before. You just missed it! Yet even if you stay here for weeks, chances are you will not see a tiger the whole time. (But that doesn't mean the tigers don't see you.)

In the morning, mist rises off the salty rivers. The trees look silvery green. At night, the water sometimes glows with tiny sea creatures who can make their own light, and the forest flashes with fireflies.

It gives you the feeling you are visiting an enchanted land. And perhaps this land really does have its own magic. The people who live here will tell you it does.

The name of the forest is Sundarbans (pronounced "SHUN-dar-bun.") The name may come from the Bengali word for beautiful, *sundar*, or from the slender, silvery sundri trees that grow here, or it may have come from the Bengali word *sumandraban*, which means "forests of ocean." No one knows. But this is just one of many mysteries here.

Sundarbans is the kind of place where things seem to disappear before your eyes. A pink fin appears suddenly in the middle of the brown river—a pink dolphin. But a second later, it vanishes beneath the water. On the beaches, little red crabs scuttle in small groups—until they spot you watching them, and then they bury themselves in the sand in the blink of an eye.

The people who live here will tell you that the tigers, too, can become invisible. They say the tigers can come out of nowhere. They say the tigers can grow to twice their normal size before your eyes—and that a person caught in a tiger's jaws shrinks. All of this sounds impossible. But then, Sundarbans is a place where the impossible seems to happen every day.

The land itself is constantly changing. Twice a day, when the tide rises, salty seawater floods the islands, sandbars, and forests. If you leave from one spot in your little boat at high tide, the trees along the river will be half submerged in water. When you return in the afternoon, you won't recognize the place: the water has drained away from the rivers, and the trees seem to have run off—now they are hundreds of yards away from the river's edge.

On the Bangladeshi side of Sundarbans, map makers have to make new maps every three years. They must draw in new islands that weren't there before and redraw shorelines in new shapes that have been sculpted by the ocean tides.

Most land plants would drown standing in so much water half the day. They would get knocked over by the tides or be poisoned by the salty water. But one group of trees and shrubs, called mangroves, has evolved ways to survive in the difficult conditions of tidal shores.

Some of the trees seem to be standing on tiptoe, as if they really are planning to sneak away once you turn your back. They have special roots called stilt roots, which help steady the trees against the tides—just as you would spread your legs wide apart to keep from being knocked over by the waves in the ocean. Woody spikes rise up from the mud. Some are fat, like spears, others as thin as pencil points. These, too, are tree roots—but they're growing up toward the sky instead of down toward the ground! Scientists call these spiky roots "pneumatophores," or "breathing roots."

The closer you look, the longer you stay, the stranger things seem in Sundarbands. Even nature doesn't seem to obey the rules.

Sometimes you can see something wet moving among the

lower branches of the mangroves. Focus your binoculars: there are fish in the trees! All of the creatures here, from the fish to the trees, the birds, and the tigers, have adapted to the special conditions of the tides that rise and fall and flush the rivers with seawater. The deer and the tigers have learned to drink saltwater. Some fish, the mudskippers, have learned to survive for many hours out of water.

Mangrove forests are special places, full of life. Sundarbans teems with strange and beautiful animals. The trees are alive with all kinds of birds: big black cormorants, with their long snaky necks; elegant white egrets; kingfishers with red bills that gleam like rubies in the sun. The waters are rich with fish. The baby fish take shelter in the stilt roots and pneumatophores of

Left, cormorants; *top right,* kingfisher; *middle right,* egret; *bottom right,* eagle.

the mangroves. The fish provide food for dolphins, birds, and people. Even the tigers occasionally eat fish.

It is a beautiful place, but dangerous. Watch out! Sundarbans is also the home of estuarine crocodiles, the most deadly crocodiles in the world. They are exactly the color of the water, and they will eat almost anything that moves—so don't go wading in the crocodile-colored rivers. There are nine different kinds of dangerous sharks. Poisonous sea snakes swim with flattened, paddlelike tails. Though they seldom bite, their venom is many times more deadly than that of a cobra.

But the creature most feared in Sundarbans is the tiger. This is the only mangrove forest with tigers in it—tigers who behave unlike any other tigers on earth.

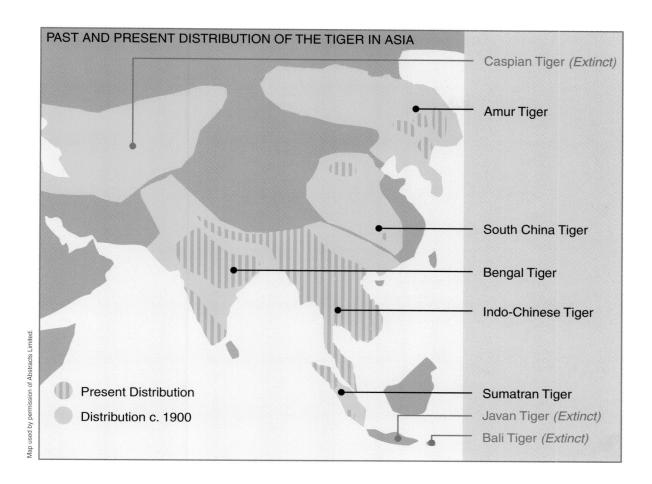

PAST AND PRESENT DISTRIBUTION OF THE TIGER IN ASIA

Caspian Tiger *(Extinct)*

Amur Tiger

South China Tiger

Bengal Tiger

Indo-Chinese Tiger

Sumatran Tiger

Javan Tiger *(Extinct)*

Bali Tiger *(Extinct)*

Present Distribution

Distribution c. 1900

Map used by permission of Abstracts Limited.

How Tigers Live

We've all heard the saying that the lion is the king of the jungle. But that's the African jungle. Tigers don't live in Africa. They live on a different continent—Asia. And in Asia's jungles, as well as its tall grasslands and even its snowy tundras, the tiger reigns supreme.

From your pet house cat to the fast-running cheetahs of Africa to the spotted jaguars prowling South American jungles, there are thirty-seven separate kinds, or species, of cats on earth. The tiger is the biggest of them all. The largest, the Siberian tiger, is a real giant: it can grow to ten feet long and can weigh eight hundred pounds. That's three hundred pounds more than a big male lion!

And the tiger is the most spectacularly beautiful of the big cats. Several of the big cats — such as the leopard, jaguar, and cheetah — have handsome spots. Lions, bobcats, and cougars are a nice tawny color. But only the tiger has a coat with amazing stripes: orange and black and white, like the flames of a fire. "Tiger, tiger, burning bright, in the forest of the night," wrote the poet William Blake. And here's something else amazing: the tiger uses this spectacular coat to make itself invisible. As unlikely as it sounds, the striped tiger, stealthily stalking its prey in tall grass or among the crisscrossing leaves of a bamboo forest, blends in so well with its background that not even a sharp-eyed deer can see it . . . till it's too late!

Perhaps this is the reason people are so excited by tigers: they seem to do and be the impossible. For instance: have you ever tried to give your pet cat a bath? Most cats hate water. Fortunately, you won't ever have to give a tiger a bath. Tigers bathe themselves. They *love* to swim. Tigers are such good swimmers that, in Sundarbans, they will even swim out into the ocean waves and swim from the country of India to the country of Bangladesh.

Tigers are great athletes. They can leap more than thirty feet in a single bound. They can walk for fifty miles without getting tired. They can climb trees. They can see in the dark. And, like almost all cats, tigers have claws that can flash out of their sheaths like switchblades to help them hold prey. (Keeping the claws sheathed most of the time allows the cat to keep them sharp.) Add to that canine teeth as long as railroad spikes, and you've got one serious predator.

How do tigers hunt? Unlike lions, tigers usually hunt alone, at night. A mother tiger teaches her cubs how to do it. It's hard work, and young tigers stay with their mothers for two years learning the tricks of the tiger trade.

A tiger usually covers about twelve miles in a night of hunting—and sometimes much more. Once the tiger has found its prey—a deer, for instance—the tiger sneaks up on the unsuspecting animal from the back or the side. Crouching cautiously, the tiger approaches slowly and soundlessly.

Finally it arrives within twenty yards of the deer. The tiger springs! The big cat's

forepaws and claws rake at the deer, knocking it off its feet. Often a single bite to the back of the neck kills the deer instantly. And then the tiger drags its hard-earned meal off into the underbrush, where it can eat in peace. A tiger can eat 77 pounds of meat in a single night, the equivalent of 140 steaks in one meal.

But tigers often must go hungry for days at a time. It's not easy being a tiger. In fact, although they can live for thirty years in the wild, most don't make it to their second birthday.

Hunting is dangerous work. A tiger might have to try ten or even twenty times before it catches a meal. The prey animals are swift, wary, and strong. The big Indian deer called sambar, for instance, can weigh seven hundred pounds, with antlers that can stretch to fifty inches. A wild boar, like those hunted by tigers in Sundarbans, has razor-sharp tusks as well as sharp hooves. Imagine how brave, how careful, and how skilled you would have to be to kill, with only your mouth and your claws, a strong animal who is fighting for its life!

Compare how hard that is with how easy it might be for a tiger to kill a person. We're far slower than most wild animals. Our senses aren't as sharp. And we have no antlers, no tusks, no hooves; we don't even have tough skin to chew through or thick hair to protect us.

Considering all that, what's most amazing about tigers is not that they sometimes eat people but that most of the time they *don't*. In fact, except in Sundarbans, healthy tigers almost *never* bother people.

One wildlife biologist tells the story of a child he met in Nepal. The little boy wandered out of his village and into the tall grass of a tiger reserve. There he stumbled upon a sleeping tiger in the grass. The tiger woke up, annoyed, and roared. But the boy was too young to take the hint. Fortunately, the tiger was a gentleman. When the little boy wouldn't leave, the tiger got up and ran away.

Rarely do tigers become man-eaters. (Most so-called man-eaters are really woman- and child-eaters. Women, who often work bending over as they wash laundry or harvest crops, make easy targets. And when children run in play, the motion is as irresistible to a tiger as a jiggling string is to a kitten. A tiger might even mistake a child for a monkey. So if you see a tiger, stand your ground — *don't run!*)

When a tiger does start eating people, though, everyone's in for big trouble. One tigress

killed 236 people in India and 200 people in Nepal before being shot by the famous hunter Jim Corbett in around 1910.

Jim Corbett made a career of tracking down and shooting dangerous tigers like her. He found that every single one of the man-eaters he killed was alike in one important way: every one was sick or injured.

Some were very old and skinny. Some had broken teeth. A few had been injured by a porcupine quill in the face or the paw. But most had been injured by a bullet. Someone had tried to kill the tiger, probably for the skin, and had only hurt it. So the injured tiger wasn't fast enough or strong enough to catch its normal prey. What else could it eat? A tiger can't eat vegetables for dinner. You guessed it: people forced most of these man-eaters to turn to eating people.

Even if you added up all the people that sick tigers were forced to eat, you wouldn't get close to the number of tigers killed by people. At the turn of the nineteenth century, tigers lived all over Asia, from the steaming rain forests of Java to the Russian Far East.

In India alone, there were forty thousand tigers—ten times more than there are today. Tigers were so common that two rich men who hunted for sport managed to kill two thousand tigers in their spare time.

There used to be eight types of tigers. Now they are only five. Three kinds are extinct—gone forever, like the dinosaurs. The five tiger subspecies that remain are all endangered—they could be next to disappear. People shoot them for their coats. They cut down the forests where tigers live, sell the logs, and move in on the tigers' land. And some people kill tigers to use their bones, blood, and even their body organs. Some people think that because tigers are strong and brave, if they have a charm from a tiger or take a medicine made from tiger parts, it will make them strong and brave, too. But of course, that doesn't work. It only robs the world of tigers.

Today, there may be only two hundred Siberian tigers left in the wild. Perhaps only six hundred fifty Sumatran tigers, with their close-set black stripes, survive on the tropical island that gives those tigers their name. Only about thirty to sixty South China tigers, with reddish coats, are left. The Indo-Chinese tiger is now down to about one thousand animals.

A tiger tooth amulet.

Most of the world's wild tigers are Royal Bengals—the kind that live in the countries of Nepal, Myanmar (formerly known as Burma), Bhutan, India, and Bangladesh. Royal Bengals' coats are usually reddish yellow to rust brown, but some, like the white tigers you may have seen in a zoo or a circus, have white coats with black stripes. (White tigers aren't what scientists call a subspecies, like Siberian or Indo-Chinese tigers. They are just Royal Bengal tigers who happen to be white with black stripes.)

The tigers who live in Sundarbans are Royal Bengals, as are all the tigers in India. And yet they behave completely differently from other Royal Bengal tigers. No other tigers live in a mangrove swamp. Nowhere else on earth do healthy tigers routinely hunt people. In fact, no other predators—not sharks, not lions, not polar bears—kill as many people a year as do the Bengal tigers of Sundarbans. Some three hundred people a year are killed by these tigers, and no one knows why.

But some people have some ideas.

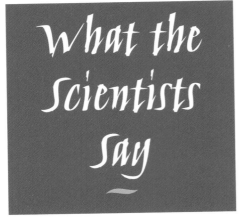

any people who travel to tiger country worry that they might run into a tiger. But scientists studying these animals worry that they won't.

In most of the places where they live, tigers are difficult to find. Tigers live by stealth. With their camouflaged coats, they are often hard to see, even if they're nearby. Even at the zoo, you can't always find the tiger in its exhibit. And in the wild, you'd have to be really lucky to see a tiger doing something important, like hunting. To see a tiger make a kill, you'd have to be as stealthy as a tiger (to avoid scaring away its prey) and warier than the prey.

Scientists who study animals like deer, ducks, or monkeys can watch many individuals at once. These animals live in herds, flocks, or troupes. But tigers usually live alone. A tigress stays with her two to three cubs for about two years. Courting pairs of tigers travel together for several days. But mostly, you can only watch one tiger at a time. If you want to study tigers, you have to be patient—like George Schaller.

He was the first American wildlife biologist to study tigers in depth. From 1963 to 1965 he studied tigers and the deer they ate in Kanha National Park in central India. Kanha is a great green and gold expanse of bamboo forest, tall grasslands, and deep ravines. There the scientist learned to recognize eleven different tigers on sight by the distinctive patterns of stripes on each one. In two years, he saw them for only 129 hours.

Most of what Schaller learned came from following their footprints, examining their kills, and even analyzing their droppings, or, as scientists call animal droppings, "scats." It is easier to find tiger scats than to find a tiger. Unlike house cats, who bury their scats, tigers often leave these calling cards in prominent places. Often you can figure out what a tiger ate by picking through its scat and analyzing the bits of hair and bone in it. If you find monkey hair in a tiger dropping, for instance, you know the tiger just ate a monkey. (And what if you find a gold bracelet or a silver earring?)

George Schaller learned how to read tiger footprints, or pugmarks, the way a person reads a book. By looking at a pugmark, Schaller could tell if the tiger was male or female. The male's hind foot is squarer than that of a female; a tigress's toes are often longer. He could tell from the pugmarks how fast the tiger was traveling. By the way the pugmarks age—they become more blurry at the edges as time goes by—he could tell how long ago the tiger passed by.

From these and other clues, Schaller figured out important facts about the tigers of central India. They avoided meeting other tigers. They hunted by night and rested during the cool of the day. They ate mainly deer.

A second and larger tiger study began in 1973 at Royal Chitawan National Park, a forest and grassland in Nepal. Those researchers added a new, high-tech tool to the study of tigers: radio telemetry.

If they found a tiger, they would shoot it with a dart gun containing a drug to make the tiger sleep. While the tiger slept, they attached a special collar to its neck that transmitted a radio signal they could follow with a hand-held radio receiver equipped with an antenna. In this way, researchers can find out exactly when a tiger is on the move, when it is sleeping, and where it travels. And the more tigers you radio-collar, the more tigers you can follow — even many tigers at once.

The researchers made an important discovery: each tiger holds a territory, the way people own land around their houses. The tiger owns this land and all the riches on it — the good sleeping places, the good hiding places, and all the deer and wild hogs who live there, too.

The tiger really is like a king or a queen who reigns over the land it owns. Except when a tigress is caring for cubs or when a male and female meet to mate, no other tigers are allowed. Each tiger patrols its territory regularly. It is not just hunting for food; it is making sure no other tigers come in.

So tigers make a point of leaving their own individual scent on trees, rocks, and bushes. These smelly signposts act as "keep out" signs to other tigers. Sometimes they rub their cheeks on an object to do this, just as your house cat does. Sometimes they mark their territories with scats. Often they mark with squirted urine, which smells sort of like buttered popcorn. Every tiger in an area knows every other tiger by scent. That's how they manage to avoid one another when they want to, and how they come together when it's time to mate.

At least that's how tigers live in two of the areas where they have been studied. But Sundarbans is different.

Sundarbans is not a grassland or a forest like Kanha or Chitawan but a salty, flooded mangrove swamp. And this poses special problems for the tigers who live there — problems that might force them to become extra ferocious.

Here are some ideas various researchers have considered over the years to explain the man-eaters of Sundarbans.

◆ In Sundarbans most of the land is slippery and sticky. Tigers elsewhere have a hard enough time hunting without having to run down their prey in sticky, gooey mud. Maybe the tigers turn to hunting people because they are easier to catch.

◆ Tigers elsewhere maintain their territories by scent-marking. But what if your scent gets washed away all the time by the tides? It would be as if someone kept ripping down

your "keep off" signs every day. You'd get in a pretty bad mood. Perhaps this makes Sundarbans tigers extraordinarily aggressive about defending the land they own against intruders—even people.

◆ Other tigers have fresh water to drink. But in Sundarbans, all the water is tinged with salt. That might make the tigers sick. Sickness could make the tigers more aggressive and also make them seek out people as easy prey.

◆ Sundarbans is full of fishermen. Maybe the tigers learned from them to associate people with food. One way people fish in Sundarbans is to string a net across a narrow channel and wait for the fish to get caught as the tide recedes. Maybe tigers learned to raid fishermen's nets—and then decided to cut out the middleman and just eat the fishermen instead!

All of these are ideas, not answers. Scientists call such ideas hypotheses. Which ones seem most likely to you?

Ideas don't solve mysteries. But they are a start. What comes next? You'll have to be inventive as you think up ways to test your hypotheses, because you can't study tigers in Sundarbans the way you would study them elsewhere.

Why not? You can't put radio collars on Sundarbans tigers as researchers did in Nepal, for the tigers here are almost never far from water. In fact, most people who see a tiger see it swimming in a river. Tigers aren't very likely to let you put a radio collar on them unless you dart them with a sleeping drug—but what would happen if you darted a swimming tiger? You guessed it: the tiger would drown.

You can't track the tigers in Sundarbans the way Schaller tracked tigers in Kanha. Sure, there are tracks everywhere. There! You can see them from your boat. You can tell from the direction the toes are facing that here a wet tiger hauled itself out of the water. In fact, it may be hiding among the mangrove trees, only fifty yards from your boat.

But you can't very well follow them. Unlike the scientists working in open, grassy areas, you would have to walk through sucking mud. With each step, you would sink up to your calves—sometimes up to your knees. Not a great place to get stuck when a tiger might leap out of hiding at any moment to eat you!

So how can you study an animal you can't see, can't track, and can't radio-collar?

You're going to need help. But fortunately, the best experts on Sundarbans tigers are living in the neat little mud-and-thatch houses at the edge of the forest. And they're a lot easier to interview than tigers.

What the Villagers Say

Meet Girindra Nath Mridha. (You pronounce his first name gee-REEN-druh.) In the fifty-foot-long wooden boat he made by hand, he has traveled the rivers, channels, and islands of Sundarbans since he was very young. He's fortunate. Unlike many of the fishermen here who paddle their little boats, he has a big boat with a motor. You're safe with him and can travel fast. Maybe you'll even see a tiger.

While you chug up and down the rivers, you can learn a lot about tigers even if you don't see one, for Girindra knows all about them. In fact, three of his uncles were eaten by tigers. He was there when his youngest uncle was killed.

Girindra tells the story: One day, when he was a young man, he went out with his youngest uncle and two others to cut wood. The biggest trees were in the tiger reserve. "It's illegal to cut wood there," Girindra explains in Bengali, "but I was young and with older members of the family, and we went anyway. I didn't know any better then.

"We dropped anchor and waded ashore," Girindra continues, "and chopped the wood with our axes. We were in a hurry. We didn't want to get caught." Park rangers sometimes patrol the big reserve to make sure people don't fish or cut down trees or collect honey illegally and disturb the wilderness. But, as the woodcutters were to learn, there are worse things than being caught by the park rangers—like being caught by a tiger.

Girindra's uncle was loading wood onto the boat when suddenly a huge tiger lurched out of the water! Girindra dove overboard. But the tiger had already grabbed Girindra's uncle by the neck and, as easily as a cat carries a mackerel, leapt overboard and swum away before anyone could help.

Almost everyone in Sundarbans knows someone who was killed by a tiger. In fact, some villages are known as Tiger Widow Villages because almost all of the women have lost a father, brother, uncle, son, or husband to a tiger. Girindra's oldest son, Sonaton (pronounce it SHONE-a-tone), is really his cousin, the son of the uncle who was killed by the tiger. Girindra adopted Sonatan, who is now fourteen, when he was too young to remember. Keen-eyed Sonaton often travels with Girindra on the boat, and he helps keep a lookout for tigers. In fact, he's often the first one to notice tiger tracks on the riverbanks. When he

Left: Sonaton on Girindra's boat. *Right*: Girindra and his wife Namita have prepared lunch for a visitor.

Girindra's neighbors gather in the yard to mend a fishing net.

spots a pugmark, he calls out "Bagh!" (that's "Tiger!" in Bengali) and points at it with a big smile full of excitement.

Girindra can take you back to his village and show you his house, which he built himself from mud and wood; the walls and floor are smooth, neat, and cool. There you can meet the rest of his family: his mother, Mabisaka; his wife, Namita; and their five girls and two boys, who are much younger than Sonaton. You would say hello with the typical Bengali greeting: "Namascar!" (NOM-ahs-CAR!) He might invite you for a fish and rice dinner at his house. (But don't expect a knife and fork. Here people eat their food with the right hand. It sounds messy, but Girindra can show you how. Afterward you can wash your hands in the rainwater pond in front of the house.)

Girindra could introduce you to other people in his village. You could talk to them and

write down some of their stories in a notebook, so you could consider all the details carefully.

Here are some of their stories:

"We had gone deep into the forest to cut wood," says Nironjan Mondol. "There were five of us. We had just left the boat." Young Nironjon was still tying the boat to a tree when a tiger came out of nowhere, flew through the air, and carried his brother off by the neck.

Montu Halda had been fishing all day with his father, brother, and brother-in-law. The tragedy struck when they thought they were safe. "Our eyes were toward the forest, where the trees were thick," says Montu. "We were expecting that if danger came, it would come from the forest." They'd finished fishing and were heading home when his brother-in-law insisted they stop and collect firewood from the forest. They kept their backs to the river, watching the forest. But the tiger approached from the river. The tiger bounded from the water and leapt onto the brother-in-law's back. He grabbed him by the neck and disappeared into the forest.

You might think that the people of Sundarbans would hate tigers. You might even think they would try to kill them all. But if you asked the people who told you the stories, they would say no.

"I would never try to hurt a tiger!" says Girindra. "We need tigers in the forest!"

"It would be terrible if the tigers were all dead!" says Nironjan.

But—aren't they afraid of the tigers?

"Yes!" says Girindra.

"Everyone fears the tiger," agrees Nironjan.

The people of Sundarbans all fear the tigers—but they don't hate them. Again, one mystery leads to another and another:

Go over the details of the stories in your notebook. The people say that the tigers can appear from nowhere and can fly through the air. Can this really be true?

A few things are for sure, though. If you look over all the stories of the Sundarbuns tigers you have collected, you'll notice that everyone agrees on several points.

First, these really are *man*-eating tigers; they don't eat women or children.

Second, the attacks occur in the forest and the rivers—not in the villages, where the women and children stay. Only the men travel far from the village and go into the forest to fish, cut wood, and collect honey. (That may be the reason the tigers eat men—and not that men just taste better.)

Third, the tigers attack from the back—just as they do when hunting deer.

This last observation gave some scientists ideas for protecting people from tiger attacks. One was the tiger guard headgear, which was sort of like a bicycle helmet that would protect the back of the neck. One design had big spikes coming out of the back. The problem was that the helmet was uncomfortable and hot. Imagine wearing it in the ninety-degree heat of the dry season!

Another design was a mask—but instead of wearing it on your face, as you would for Halloween, you wear this mask on the back of the head. Why? Because that way the tigers can't figure out where your back is—and they seldom attack from the front. These

masks are available to everyone in Sundarbans. Oddly, most people don't wear them. Maybe they are making a silly mistake, like people in the United States who don't wear seatbelts in their cars.

But the people of Sundarbans have other ways to protect themselves: they tell stories and say prayers.

Tiger God of the Jungle

What kind of story can protect you from tigers?

Girindra will be happy to tell you. Everyone in Sundarbans, even the littlest child, knows the story of Daskin Ray, the Tiger God, and Bonobibi, the Forest Goddess. Daskin Ray (DAW-kin ROY) means "Lord of the South" in Bengali.

"It happened long ago," Girindra begins, "when Daskin Ray first came to rule the forest of Sundarbans."

He was a great ruler: handsome, brave, and powerful—so powerful that he could turn himself into a tiger.

Daskin Ray owned all the riches of the forest. He owned the trees that people use to build their houses and light their fires and that shelter the shores from cyclones. He owned the fish that everyone eats every day. He owned the delicious honey made by the bees who live wild in the forest.

Daskin Ray was a kind ruler. He shared these riches with the people. But if they failed to pay him tribute—if they were ungrateful and used his gifts unwisely—Daskin Ray would send an army of tigers, crocodiles, and sharks to punish them.

"For many years, Daskin Ray ruled Sundarbans' beautiful forests and rivers alone," Girindra says. "And then one day, newcomers arrived." The most important of these was a baby girl whose mother was lost in the forest on the very day she was going to give birth. She had to give birth in the jungle, alone. She had two babies, a boy and a girl. The mother could carry only one baby with

her as she tried to find her way through the forest back to her village. She took the boy and, sadly, left the girl behind.

Some little chital deer found the baby girl. Feeling sorry for her, the deer decided to raise her. They taught her the ways of the jungle. She grew to know its magic. The girl, named Bonobibi, grew up to become a goddess with special powers. Crocodiles and sharks would obey her commands. She could protect both people and animals. She considered all the creatures of the forest her children.

Naturally, Daskin Ray was at first jealous of her powers. In fact, he went to war against Bonobibi. Daskin Ray changed into a tiger, and when he slunk into the river he ordered his army of crocodiles and sharks to attack. But they couldn't hurt Bonobibi because she was too powerful. So Daskin Ray, the Tiger God, and Bonobibi, the Forest Goddess, stopped fighting and made a pact of friendship. "And from that day onward," says Girindra, "they have ruled the forest together in peace."

So have the people of Sundarbans lived together in peace through the centuries. Some are followers of the Hindu religion, with its many different images of gods and goddesses, sometimes shown with extra arms or blue skin. Others follow the Muslim religion and call their god by the name Allah. Elsewhere in India and Bangladesh and in Pakistan, Hindus and Muslims sometimes fight, as Bonobibi and Daskin Ray once did. But in Sundarbans, Hindus and Muslims worship side by side at the shrines to honor the Tiger God and the Forest Goddess.

Every village has these shrines, and Girindra will take you to one. You can even find little shrines built right in the forest. Inside, you might see a clay statue of Bonobibi. She is very beautiful,

Bonobibi, the Forest Goddess.

dressed in a long dress and wearing pretty jewelry and maybe a crown. Daskin Ray sometimes appears as a tiger. Sometimes he has the head of a tiger and the feet of a man. And sometimes he is shown as a man riding a tiger.

But this clay image isn't meant to show that Daskin Ray rides on tigers the way you ride a bicycle. Instead, the artist wants to show you that the tiger *carries* the god the way a breeze might carry a perfume, the way a speech carries a message, the way your voice carries a tune.

The sculptor of the image is trying to make an important point: any tiger you see in the forest might carry the very spirit of Daskin Ray. Any tiger in the forest might well carry the power that still protects the Sundarbans forest to this day. To show their respect for the Tiger God and the

Daskin Ray, the Tiger God.

Forest Goddess, people often leave little presents in front of the statues: a coin or some incense, a fruit or a flower. Maybe you will want to leave something, too.

The people of Sundarbans consider this story so important that each February it is re-told at a special ceremony. If you visit in February, you may get to come along.

A priest sings the story of Bonobibi and Daskin Ray. The singing goes on all day. Everyone wears their finest clothes. People celebrate with music and sweet-smelling incense, flowers and special foods. Sculptors create brand-new statues of Bonobibi and

Daskin Ray and other characters in the story and set them in a shrine. People make offerings at the feet of the statues to show how grateful they are that Bonobibi and Daskin Ray still share their riches with them. They pray to the Tiger God to protect them. Then everyone eats a big meal together.

It sounds like fun, and it is. But the ceremony isn't just an excuse for a big party. The point is to listen again to the story so that nobody ever forgets it.

Why is this story so important?

Girindra will tell you: "Because it's true!"

Tiger Magic

How can the story of the Tiger God be true?

It sounds like a fairy tale: an exciting story full of fantasy and magic, but not something that really happened — much less something that is still happening today. Many people would dismiss these beliefs about tigers as silly superstitions.

But maybe we have overlooked something.

Meet Rathin (row-TEEN) Banerjee. He's one of the directors of the Forest Department in Sundarbans. He's responsible for the forest guards who patrol against intruders in the wilderness of the tiger reserve. People are allowed to fish and collect honey and cut trees around their own villages, but in the tiger reserve, no one is allowed to cut the trees or catch the fish or collect the honey without special permission.

Naturally, some people try to sneak in anyway. Some people everywhere break the law—even when everyone agrees that the laws protect people and animals alike.

It might not seem that a few people cutting down trees or collecting honey or fishing in the tiger reserve would do anybody any harm. But Rathin explains that all of these activities disturb the mangrove forest—especially cutting down trees.

Who needs mangrove forests, anyway? The tigers and deer,

Top: Rathin plots a course aboard the Forest Department boat, *Monorama*. *Bottom*: A Forest Department guard stands ready to protect Sundarbans's forest.

the turtles and dolphins, the crabs and the birds do. The people of Sundarbans do, too—
and they know it.

If it weren't for the mangrove forests, Rathin explains, the baby fish couldn't take shelter among the strange stilt roots and breathing roots at high tide. If the fish were gone,
the people would have nothing to eat. And the mangroves shelter the people, too.
Remember those cyclones that blow apart houses? The damage would be far worse if the
trees weren't there to break the force of the winds. In fact, the winds would probably
blow everything away.

That's why Rathin's job is so important. In fact, all around the world most of the mangrove forests that once covered coastlines are now gone. Sundarbans is the largest one left.
Rathin and his staff work hard to keep intruders away, to prevent fishermen and honey

collectors and woodcutters from felling all the trees in the tiger reserve. "But Sundarbans is too big for us to protect it all," admits Rathin.

Fortunately, though, the Forest Department has help: five hundred man-eating tigers! Who could ask for better forest guards than that?

"Because the forest is full of these dangerous man-eaters," Rathin says, "far fewer poachers even try to penetrate the tiger reserve to cut wood."

The old stories warn that if you fail to respect the tiger's territory, there may be terrible consequences. And this is true. Remember, the tigers don't come into the villages: 90 percent of the tiger attacks happen inside the tiger reserve.

Clay images of honey collectors in some of the shrines remind villagers that Daskin Ray owns the wild bees and honey.

Perhaps one of those scientific theories is right. Maybe these tigers, whose territorial scent marks are washed away daily, really are superterritorial. When they attack people, perhaps they're trying to protect the land that they own.

And maybe, as the ancient legends say, the tiger really is watching over the forest—for everyone's benefit.

But what about some of the other things the villagers say? Can tigers really fly through the air? Can they become invisible? Do people whom tigers catch really shrink in their jaws? It sounds impossible.

And yet these stories are told by people who have carefully watched tigers for many years. They may not have college degrees, as the scientists do. But they have spent many more hours among tigers than most scientists here. And their lives literally depend on how well they can predict how tigers will behave.

To dismiss what the villagers say as silly or wrong or just superstition could be a big mistake. Sure, they might be wrong—anyone can make a mistake. But they may well be telling the truth—perhaps a truth they understand in a different way than we would.

Stories about animals that seem far-fetched often turn out to be true. The Chippewa

For centuries, Asian artists have portrayed tigers' power and grace in beautiful artwork like this temple mural.

Indians of America's Great Lakes, for instance, believed that spider webs protected babies by "catching the harm in the air." Mothers hoped that a spider would weave a web over her baby's cradle; if one didn't, the parent would collect a web on a hoop and hang it over the baby.

Sound crazy? Actually it was a wise idea. A scientist, Joe Raver, points out that spider webs make excellent mosquito netting. And in an area full of biting mosquitoes and black flies, the webs protected babies from bug-borne diseases, itchy mosquito bites, and other insect-carried "harm in the air." The story turns out to be true after all!

Sometimes it's downright dangerous not to pay attention to the stories people tell about animals. There was an old saying in the American West that "a rattlesnake doesn't die until sundown." How could that be? The saying was meant to remind people that even a dead snake can kill you. The snake's venom remains in its fangs even when it's dead. In fact,

one in ten people who are "bitten" by poisonous snakes are actually poisoned by the venom in the fangs of dead snakes they unwisely handled.

Here's another story: Some people who live near Florida's swamps say the crocodiles there will grab you by your shadow, pull you into the water, and eat you. (These animals are true crocodiles, not Florida alligators, which are more gentle.) The longer the shadow, people warn, the more aggressive the crocodile is likely to be. The story comes from keen observation. As one researcher recently noted, if your shadow touches the water's edge, you're close enough for a crocodile to grab you.

And this is the case with the villagers' stories of Sundarbans tigers. Maybe the tigers don't fly through the air like Tinkerbell. But a tiger *can* leap thirty feet in a single bound—as if they *are* flying. You can't see through a tiger as if it were some cartoon ghost. But it *can* become invisible—after all, even in the zoo you often can't see a tiger hidden behind a single blade of grass. And maybe human bodies don't really shrink in the jaws of the tiger. But when a tiger picks up a person at the back of the neck, the body curves into a comma shape and certainly looks smaller.

Sometimes what is true is hidden, as in a riddle. Here's one: when are man-eating tigers really life-saving protectors? You guessed it: when they guard the forest on which every-one depends.

There are many ways to find hidden truths—that's what solving mysteries is all about. Sometimes you find them by watching, the way Schaller watched the tigers in Kanha. Sometimes you find them by doing scientific experiments. Sometimes you can find truths by listening to stories. And sometimes you need to do all three: watch, experiment, and listen.

Lots of important truths are hidden in the stories people tell about tigers in Sundar-bans—truths about how we ought to behave on this earth. Long before American sci-entists started studying tigers and learning the secrets of how they live, the people of Sundarbans knew one of the most important things about them: our world can't be whole without tigers. We need to protect tigers, because even dangerous, man-eating tigers may do us more good than harm.

On one of the days when you are traveling with Girindra and Sonaton, perhaps you will be lucky. Maybe it will happen as you are relaxing on the deck after a lunch of rice and crab. As you round a bend in the river, suddenly Sonaton's arm shoots out. He calls out, "Bagh!"

For a second it looks like a rock: a roundish object in the middle of the brown river, a rim of white water foaming at its edge. But this rock is moving! The rock is a head—the face of a tiger—swimming across the river at right angles to the path of the boat.

Because the tiger's body is wet, it may look black in the water. But the head is the color of a flame. The tiger may not even look at you. It only wants to cross the river. Within seconds it reaches the bank. The tiger climbs out onto the mud, water sheeting off its fur, and slips into the forest. It seems to disappear into thin air, as invisible—and yet as real—as your own breath.

Let's Speak Bengali

Bengali is a beautiful language known for its great poetry. It is just one of more than one hundred languages spoken in India along with Hindi and Urdu. Bengali is the official language of the Indian state of West Bengal and the nation of Bangladesh.

Bengali is distantly related to the English language, but it has different rules. Often the order of words in sentences seems to be backward. For instance, if you wanted to say, "Why are there so many people at your sister's house?" the words would be in this order: "In the house of your sister, so many people, why?"

Here are some sentences you might want to learn before you visit West Bengal or Bangladesh:

Greetings!	Namaskar! (NOM-ahs-CAR!)
What is your name? (Your name is what?)	Apnar nam ki? (Ahp-nar NAHM ki?)
My name is Bob. (My name Bob.)	Amar nam Bob. (Amar nahm Bob.)
I live in America. (I America live in.)	Ami America thaki. (Ah-MEE uh-MER-ica ta-KEE.)
I speak Bengali. (I Bengali speak.)	Ami Bangla boli. (Ah-MEE Bang-LA bolee.)
Where is the tiger? (Tiger where?)	Bagh kothai? (Bog ko-TIE?)
Where is the snake? (Snake where?)	Shap kothai? (Shop ko-TIE?)
Where is the crocodile? (Crocodile where?)	Kumeer kothai? (Koo-MEER ko-TIE?)
Sundarbans is very beautiful. (Sundarbans very beautiful.)	Sundarbuan khub sundar. (SHUN-dar-bun KOOB shun-dar.)
There is the tiger! (There tiger is!)	Shekane bagh ache! (SHAY-kan-ay bog ah-chay!)

Tiger Index: Some Statistics

Estimated number of wild tigers in 1900: about 70,000

Number of wild tigers today in Asia: about 7,000

Number of humans on earth in 1900: less than 2 billion

Number of humans on earth today: more than 6 billion

Number of tiger subspecies in 1900: 8*

Number of tiger subspecies today: 5

Average amount of territory a male tiger owns in Royal
  Chitawan National Park: 23–40 square miles

Average amount of territory a female tiger owns there: 8 square miles

Age to which a tiger can live: 30

Age by which most tigers die: 2

Pounds of meat a tiger can eat in one night: 77

Weight of largest subspecies of tiger (Siberian, adult male): up to 800 pounds

Weight of smallest subspecies of tiger (Sumatran, adult male): 250 pounds

Amount paid for one pound of tiger bone medicine on the black market: $500

* The last Bali tiger was killed in 1937; hunters exterminated the last Caspian tigers in the
  1970s; and the last Javan tiger died in the 1980s.

Books About Tigers

The following are written especially for kids.

Clutton-Brock, Juliet. *Eyewitness Books: World of Cats*. New York: Knopf, 1991. A leading animal expert writes about the evolution and behavior of all the cats, including tigers.

Higgins, Mana. *Cats: From Tigers to Tabbies*. New York: Crown, 1998. An overview of cats, including how they hunt and live in the wild and with people.

Stonehouse, Bernard. *A Visual Introduction to Wild Cats*. New York: Checkmark Books, 1999. You'll especially enjoy the great illustrations.

Thapar, Valmik. *Tiger*. Austin, Tex.: Raintree, 2000. The author is a well-known Indian researcher who has worked for decades studying wild Royal Bengal tigers. This book discusses their habitats, life cycle, food, and the threats facing them.

Advanced readers may want to try these books, which were written for adults.

Corbett, Jim. *The Man Eaters of Kumaon*. New York: Oxford University Press, 1946. Read about the adventures of the man who hunted down injured tigers who were forced to eat people, written by the hunter himself.

Montgomery, Sy. *Spell of the Tiger: The Man-Eaters of Sundarbans*. Boston: Houghton Mifflin, 1995. A first-person account of three expeditions to Sundarbans with Girindra, Rathin, and others.

Schaller, George. *The Deer and the Tiger: A Study of Wildlife in India*. Chicago: University of Chicago Press, 1967. The pioneering scientist's own descriptions of the first long-term study of deer and tiger in central India.

Some Organizations Helping Tigers

A number of fine organizations are trying to help tigers in different ways. Some fund researchers who study tigers in the wild. Others help captive tigers and other big cats in distress. Still others try to conserve tigers' land or fund patrols to protect against poachers.

Here are just a few organizations that you might consider supporting. Those below have newsletters and Web pages to keep you up to date.

Save the Tiger Fund

National Fish and Wildlife Foundation

1120 Connecticut Ave. NW

Suite 900

Washington, DC 20036

www.5tigers.org

The fund sponsors education, conservation, and antipoaching programs, including thirteen projects for Royal Bengal tigers in India and Nepal. One project uses hidden cameras to count and identify wild tigers. The Web site includes a Tiger Information Center maintained by the Minnesota Zoo and a special Web page, "Cubs and Kids."

Wildlife Protection Society of India

Thapar House 124, Janpath,

New Delhi, 110 001

India

Directed by Belinda Wright, a woman who grew up with tigers at Kanha in central India, this organization investigates and exposes tiger poachers and the rich men who back them. It also funds creative ways to protect the Royal Bengal tigers of India.

Hornocker Wildlife Institute

P.O. Box 3246

University of Idaho

Moscow, ID 83843

www.uidaho.edu/rsrch/hwi/stpbio.html

This serious research group is especially active in the struggle to save the Siberian tiger from extinction. It also conducts scientific projects on mountain lions and bears.

International Society for Endangered Cats

3070 Riverside Drive

Suite 160

Columbus, OH 43221

www.isec.org

This organization funds research, antipoaching projects, land conservation, and education to benefit all the big cats. It has special programs for kids.

Tiger Missing Link Foundation

Tiger Creek Wildlife Refuge

Tyler, TX

www.tigerlink.org

This organization works to help save tigers in three ways. It encourages wise management of captive populations, helps educate people about tigers (including an on-line resource, "Tiger Learning Center," which is available to schools) and rescues and rehabilitates tigers and other big cats who have been abused and neglected in captivity. Its Web site includes a special series of pages just for kids.

Wildlife Conservation Society

Bronx Zoo

Bronx, NY 10460

www.wcs.org

Sponsors studies and conservation programs for tigers, their land, and their prey in India, China, Korea, Malaysia, Thailand, Vietnam, Russia, and Myanmar (Burma). The Web site has a special Kids Only page and also lists ways *you* can take action to save tigers and wildlife around the world.

Acknowledgments

Many kind people helped me during the four expeditions I made to India to research Sundarbans and its unusual tigers. I especially thank Girindra Nath Mridha and his family: Mabisaka, Namita, Sonaton, Shumitra, Shubadra, Shushitra, Shushoma, Shoroma, Monuds, and Modhusudan. I thank all the kind people who shared their stories with me. I thank Rathin Banerjee for sharing his expertise. I thank my excellent interpreters, Soma Banerjee, Shankar Muhkerjee, Debashish Nandy, and Amarendra Nath Mondol. I thank Eleanor Briggs, who traveled with me on my second expedition and who provided the wonderful photographs in this book, and Dianne Taylor Snow, who accompanied me on my first voyage.

For helping make this book possible, I thank my friend Robert M. Oksner, my editor, Amy Flynn, and my literary agent, Sarah Jane Freymann.

A Note on the Photographs

Eleanor Briggs, the photographer, has traveled all over Asia photographing its people, places, and wildlife. She accompanied me on the second of my four expeditions to Sundarbans. She took the photographs of Royal Bengal tigers in captivity. The tiger on pages 16 and 55 had been captured wild in Sundarbans before coming to the Calcutta Zoo.

Index